Sunshine

William K. Durr
Jean M. LePere
John J. Pikulski
Susan Shaw

Consultant:
Hugh Schoephoerster

HOUGHTON MIFFLIN COMPANY   BOSTON

Atlanta   Dallas   Geneva, Illinois   Lawrenceville, New Jersey   Palo Alto   Toronto

Acknowledgments

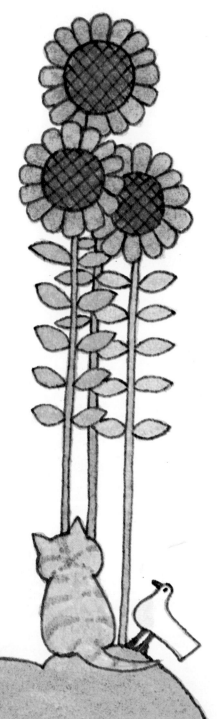

Grateful acknowledgment is given for the contributions of Paul McKee.

For each of the selections listed below, acknowledgment is made for permission to adapt and/or reprint copyrighted material, as follows:

"Abu Ali and the Coat," from *Abu Ali, Three Tales of the Middle East*, retold by Dorothy O. Van Woerkom. Copyright © 1976 by Dorothy O. Van Woerkom. Reprinted by permission of Macmillan Publishing Co., Inc., and World's Work Ltd.

"Bears," by Elizabeth Coatsworth. Copyright © 1974 by Elizabeth Coatsworth. Reprinted by permission of the author.

"Buzzy Bear and the Rainbow," from *Buzzy Bear and the Rainbow*, by Dorothy Marino. Copyright © 1962 by Dorothy Marino. Reprinted by permission of McIntosh and Otis, Inc.

"Ira Sleeps Over," from *Ira Sleeps Over*, by Bernard Waber. Copyright © 1972 by Bernard Waber. Reprinted by permission of Houghton Mifflin Company.

"Jerry's Important Things," from *The Box of Important Things*, by Ann Hellie. © 1968 by Western Publishing Company, Inc. Used by permission of the publisher.

"Lion," from *The Raucous Auk*, by Mary Ann Hoberman. Copyright © 1973 by Joseph Low. All rights reserved. Reprinted by permission of Viking Penguin, Inc.

"Pockets," from *Nuts to You and Nuts to Me*, by Mary Ann Hoberman. Copyright © 1974 by Mary Ann Hoberman. Reprinted by permission of Alfred A. Knopf, Inc., and Russell & Volkening, Inc.

"Spring Planting," from *Rhymes About the Country*, by Marchette Chute. Copyright 1941 (Macmillan). Reprinted by permission of the author.

"This Tooth," from *Kim's Place*, by Lee Bennett Hopkins. Text copyright © 1974 by Lee Bennett Hopkins. Reprinted by permission of Holt, Rinehart and Winston, Publishers, and Curtis Brown, Ltd.

Credits

Illustrators: pp. 7–15, ANDRE AMSTUTZ; pp. 16–26, JAN BRETT; pp. 27–32, DIANE PATERSON; pp. 33–42, MONICA SANTA; p. 43, MARY MACLAREN; pp. 47–62, DORA LEDER; p. 63, CLAUDETTE BOULANGER; pp. 64–65, CHRISTINE CZERNOTA; pp. 69–76, ANATOLY DVERIN; pp. 77–78, DOROTHEA SIERRA; pp. 79–94, ANGELA ADAMS; p. 95, LINDA BICK; pp. 96–100, DIANE DE GROAT; pp. 101–116, ANDRZEJ DUDZINSKI; pp. 118–127, MICHAEL HAGUE; p. 128, SUSAN CONSIDINE; pp. 133–153,

(Acknowledgments and Artist Credits are continued on page 190.)

Copyright © 1983, 1981 by Houghton Mifflin Company

All rights reserved. No part of this work may be reproduced or transmitted in any form or by any means, electronic or mechanical, including photocopying and recording, or by any information storage or retrieval system, except as may be expressly permitted by the 1976 Copyright Act or in writing by the publisher. Requests for permission should be addressed in writing to Houghton Mifflin Company, One Beacon Street, Boston, Massachusetts 02108 .

Printed in the U.S.A.

ISBN: 0-395-31937-4

Contents

Sunshine

MAGAZINE ONE

Contents

Pig Jumps

by BOB BARNER

Frog: Look at me, Pig.

See how I can jump.

Pig: That was a good jump, Frog.

How did you do it?

I want to jump like that, too.

But pigs can't jump like frogs.

Frog: I think I can help you, Pig.

Look in this box.

You will get a surprise.

Pig: Oh, good!

I like surprises.

What is it?

Frog: It will help you jump like I do.

Now look, Pig.

Look at me jump.

Pig: That was a big jump!

I want to jump like that.

Now come down, Frog.

I am going to open my surprise.

Don't you want to see me open it?

Frog: I want to see you open the box.

But now I can't get down.

Can you help me get down, Pig?

Pig: I can't jump like you, Frog.

I don't think I can get you down.

But I'll go and get help.

Frog: Don't go, Pig!

Open the box now.

Pig: I can't open the box now, Frog.

I want to get help for you.

I don't need a surprise now.

Frog: Oh, but you do, Pig.

You do need that surprise.

Pig: OK! OK!

I'll open the box.

Then I'll get help for you.

Frog: Surprise! Surprise!

Pig: Oh, thank you, Frog!
But what are they?

Frog: They go on your feet, Pig.
They will help you jump.
Now you can jump up here.
You can help me get down.

Pig: They are on my feet now.
Here I come.

Pig: Oh, Frog.

I did not make a good jump.

It was too little.

What can we do now?

Frog: Come on, Pig.

You can do it!

You can jump up here.

Make a big, big jump.

13

Pig: OK. I'll jump up to you.

Then you jump on my hat.

Here I come!

Frog: Thank you, Pig.

You did it.

Now you can jump like I do.

That was a big, big jump.

Pig: Thank you, Frog.

I did jump like you.

That was a big, big surprise!

The Big Sale

by ALMA MARSHAK WHITNEY

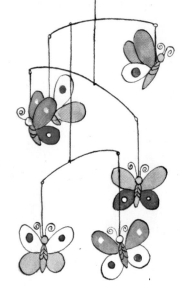

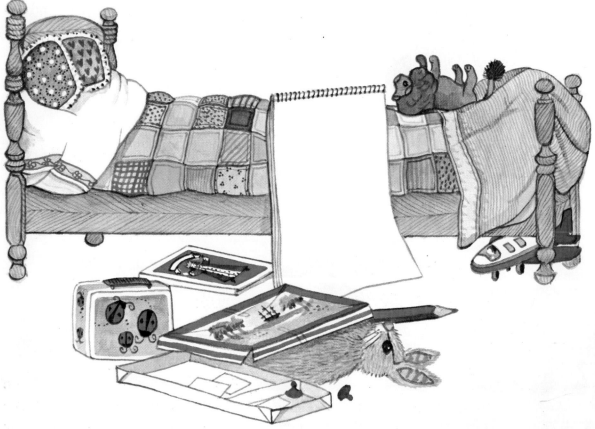

Nina: I don't need this rabbit.

I don't need this book.

And I don't need this old game.

What can I do with my things?

Can you help me, Susan?

Susan: I think I can help you.

We will need a big box.

Nina: Here is a big box.

Why do you need it?

Susan: We can put your things in this box.

I'll put this red pencil in, too.

And what is this old thing?

Nina: Oh, that's a lunch box.

You can put that in the box, too.

Susan: Look at all the things in this box!

Now we can have a big sale.

Nina: A sale?

How do we have a sale?

Susan: You will see.

Now where did I put that red pencil?

Nina: You put it in the box.

I'll get it for you.

Susan: Look at this.

We can put it on the things for sale.

Now we will take the box and go out.

Amy: Hello, Nina.

Hello, Susan.

What are you doing?

Susan: We have some things for sale.

Do you need an old lunch box?

Amy: No, I don't need a lunch box.

But I like this rabbit.

What do you want for it?

Nina: That rabbit is not for sale.

I like it, too.

James: What is all this?

Susan: It's a big sale, James.

James: Oh, look what I found.
This looks like a good game.
I'll take it.

Nina: That game is not for sale.
My father likes my games.
That's the one he likes best.

James: OK, Nina.

I'll take this book then.

I can read it to Andy.

Nina: Oh, James.

That book is not for sale.

I can read it to Jan.

She likes a story in it.

Susan: Your rabbit was not for sale.

Then your game was not for sale.

Now your book is not for sale.

You don't have *one* thing for sale!

Nina: I don't want to have a sale.

I want all my things.

Susan: OK, Nina.

I'll put the things back in the box.

Susan: I wanted to help you, Nina.

But now all your things are back.

Nina: You *did* help me, Susan.

It looks good in here now.

How Can You Tell?

Read what is in this box.

Maria: Look at my hat.

Now read what Maria said.

How can you tell Maria said this?

Maria tells you.

Now read what is in this box.

Maria said, "Look at my hat."

How can you tell Maria said this?

Maria said tells you.

How can you tell what she said?

Now read this story.

Maria said, "Look at my hat."

David said, "I like it."

"Put it on," David said.

"I don't want to," Maria said.

28

"I can help you put it on," said David.

"I can put it on," said Maria.
"But I don't want to."

"It's a good hat," said David.

"It is a good old hat," said Maria.
"I like it."

"Then put it on!" David said.

"Don't ask me to put it on," Maria said.

30

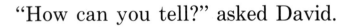

"Then can I put it on?" David asked.

"You can put it on," Maria said.

"But you will not like it."

"How can you tell?" asked David.

"Put it on and find out," said Maria.

"It's too big!" said David.

"I can't see a thing!"

"It is too big," said Maria.

"But it's a good hat for a cat."

32

The Little Red Hen

One day the little red hen said,
"Come see what I have found!
I have some wheat.
I am going to plant it."

"Who will help me plant the wheat?" asked the little red hen.

"Not I," said the duck.

"Not I," said the cat.

"Not I," said the pig.

"Then I will plant it myself,"
said the little red hen.
And she did.

The wheat grew and grew.
It grew into a big plant.

"Who will help me cut the wheat?"
asked the little red hen.

"Not I," said the duck.

"Not I," said the cat.

"Not I," said the pig.

"Then I will cut it myself,"
said the little red hen.
And she did.

"Who will help me pound the wheat?"
asked the little red hen.

"Not I," said the duck.

"Not I," said the cat.

"Not I," said the pig.

"Then I will pound it myself,"
said the little red hen.
And she did.

"I will take the wheat to the mill,"
said the little red hen.
"The mill will make the wheat into flour.
Who will help me take the wheat
to the mill?"

"Not I," said the duck.

"Not I," said the cat.

"Not I," said the pig.

"Then I will take it myself,"
said the little red hen.
And she did.

"I will make bread with the flour,"
said the little red hen.

"Who will help me make the bread?"

"Not I," said the duck.

"Not I," said the cat.

"Not I," said the pig.

"Then I will make the bread myself,"
said the little red hen.

And she did.

"Now who will help me eat the bread?" asked the little red hen.

"I will," said the duck.

"I will," said the cat.

"I will," said the pig.

"Oh, no," said the little red hen.

"You did not help me plant the wheat.

You did not help me cut the wheat.

You did not help me pound the wheat.

You did not help me take the wheat
to the mill.

You did not help me make the bread.

So you will not help me eat the bread.

I will eat it myself."

And she did.

Spring Planting

by MARCHETTE CHUTE

My garden seeds are coming up
    In the most surprising squiggles.
I planted them extremely straight,
    And then they got the wiggles.

Things That Grow

This plant is little.

It will grow to be big.

Then the plant
will look like this.

Here is a little duck.

It will grow and grow.

This is how

the duck will look.

They are little.

They will grow, too.

They will look like this.

Plants grow.

Ducks grow.

You grow.

Jerry's Important Things

by ANN HELLIE

Jerry had a box.

It was not a big box.

But it had some important things in it.

"What do you have in that box?"
asked Mother.

"Important things," said Jerry.
"You can look in the box.
But don't tell Grandmother
what is in it.
I want to surprise her."

"You *do* have important things

in the box," said Mother.

"Grandmother will like your surprise.

You may go to see her now."

So Jerry went out with the box.

Jerry saw Mr. Higgins.

"Is that box for me?" asked Mr. Higgins.

"Oh, no," said Jerry.
"My important things are in this box."

"May I see your important things?"
asked Mr. Higgins.

"You may take one look," said Jerry.

Jerry opened the box.

"They *are* important things,"
said Mr. Higgins.

"I have to go now," said Jerry.

"I am going to my grandmother's house."

51

Then Jerry saw Mrs. Hall.

"Hello, Jerry," said Mrs. Hall.
"What do you have in that box?"

"I have important things," said Jerry.
"You may take a look."

"Oh, my," said Mrs. Hall.
"You have *two* important things."

"I have to go now," said Jerry.
"I am going to surprise my grandmother."

Then Jerry saw Mr. Dobbs.

"Hello, Jerry," said Mr. Dobbs.
"Will you help me with this?"

Jerry put his box down.
He ran to help Mr. Dobbs.

"Thank you, Jerry," said Mr. Dobbs.
"I think that will do it."

"I have to go now," said Jerry.
He ran back to get his box.

"Oh, no!" said Jerry.

"My box is not here.

I can't find it."

"Tell me what it looks like,"
said Mr. Dobbs.

"It's not a very big box," said Jerry.

"But I have something important in it."

Mr. Dobbs helped Jerry look for the box.

They looked and looked.

Mr. Drew came up to Jerry and Mr. Dobbs.

"Hello," said Mr. Drew.

"What are you looking for?"

"Oh, Mr. Drew," said Jerry.

"I can't find my box.

It's not a very big box.

But it is an important box."

55

So Mr. Drew helped look, too.

Then Mrs. Downing stopped
to see what was going on.

"What are you doing?" she asked.

"We can't find my important box,"
Jerry said.

"I'll help look," said Mrs. Downing.

They all went on looking.

They looked and looked.

But no one found the box.

Then Mrs. Downing said, "I found it!

I found it!"

They all looked at Mrs. Downing.

"That's it!" said Jerry.

"That's my box!

You found it! Thank you!"

"My dog found it, too,"

said Mr. Dobbs.

"Thank you for your help," said Jerry.

"Now I have my important things.

I want you to see them."

Jerry opened the box.

"They are so little," said Mrs. Downing.

Mr. Drew said, "You will get new ones.

You will get *two* new ones."

"I have to go now," said Jerry.

"I want my grandmother to see

my important things, too."

Jerry went on to Grandmother's house.

"Hello, Jerry," said Grandmother.

"It's good to see you.

What do you have in the box?"

"I have some important things in it.

I wanted to surprise you," said Jerry.

Jerry opened the box.

"This *is* a surprise," said Grandmother.

"They are important things.

Why don't you open the box

so *everyone* can see them?"

"I will," said Jerry.

And he did!

This Tooth

by LEE BENNETT HOPKINS

I jiggled it
    jaggled it
    jerked it.
I pushed
    and pulled
    and poked it.
But —
As soon as I stopped, and left it alone,
This tooth came out on its very own!

Can You Find Them?

Can you find —

Pig and Frog?

Nina and Susan?

Little Red Hen?

Jerry?

65

Sunshine

MAGAZINE TWO

Contents

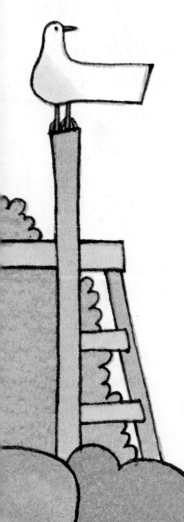

The Big Turnip

by ALEXEI TOLSTOY

One day an old man planted
a little turnip.

The little turnip grew and grew.

It grew into a very big turnip.

Then one day, the old man went
to pull up the turnip.

He pulled and pulled.

But he could not pull it up.

So he asked the old woman to help.

The old woman pulled the old man.
The old man pulled the turnip.

And they pulled and pulled.
But they could not pull it up.

So the old woman asked the little girl
to help.

The little girl pulled the old woman.
The old woman pulled the old man.
The old man pulled the turnip.

And they pulled and pulled.
But they could not pull it up.

So the little girl asked the dog to help.

The dog pulled the little girl.

The little girl pulled the old woman.

The old woman pulled the old man.

The old man pulled the turnip.

And they pulled and pulled.

But they could not pull it up.

So the dog asked the cat to help.

The cat pulled the dog.

The dog pulled the little girl.

The little girl pulled the old woman.

The old woman pulled the old man.

The old man pulled the turnip.

And they pulled and pulled.

But they could not pull it up.

So the cat asked the mouse to help.

The mouse pulled the cat.

The cat pulled the dog.

The dog pulled the little girl.

The little girl pulled the old woman.

The old woman pulled the old man.

The old man pulled the turnip.

They pulled and pulled.

And up came the turnip at last.

One Word from Two Words

Here are some things you play with.

They are **playthings.**

Look at the word **playthings.**

It is made from two words.

You can read **play** and **things.**

So you can read **playthings.**

What two words make

the word **playhouse?**

Here are more words made
from two words you can read.

The best story is in this **storybook.**

The dog likes the **doghouse.**

Pig put his hat in a **hatbox.**

Tell what two words make the words
storybook, doghouse, and **hatbox.**

Lucy
Didn't
Listen

Lucy liked school.

She liked to read.

She liked to play games.

And she liked to do school work.

But Lucy had one problem.

She did not listen.

One day Mrs. Mills said,

"Put your things away.

We will go and get some books now."

But Lucy was not listening.

She was too busy working.

Lucy looked up.

No one was in the room.

"Everyone went to lunch," she thought.

"I'll get my lunch box and go, too."

Mrs. Mills saw Lucy.

"Oh, Lucy!" she said.

"You didn't listen.

I said we were going to get books."

Lucy said, "I do listen, Mrs. Mills.

But today I was too busy working."

"Lucy, go back to the room
and get your book," said Mrs. Mills.

Pam saw Lucy coming back
from the room.

"You didn't put your lunch box away,"
said Pam.

"I was too busy getting my book,"
said Lucy.

Lucy looked for a book.

She found one she wanted to read.

Then Mrs. Mills asked, "Girls and boys, do you have your books now?"

The girls and boys said, "Yes, we do, Mrs. Mills."

Lucy was not listening.

She was too busy reading her book.

She didn't see everyone go back to the room.

When they were back in the room,

Mrs. Mills said, "Put your books away.

Then we can go out to play."

Kevin said, "Lucy is not here.

She was reading when I last saw her.

Do you want me to get her?"

"Yes," said Mrs. Mills.

"Tell her we are going out to play."

Kevin went to get Lucy.

Then they went out to play, too.

Lucy was busy reading her book.

Pam said, "Come and play a game, Lucy.

You be a squirrel.

Kevin and I will be a tree.

We are playing SQUIRREL IN THE TREE.

Mrs. Mills will tell you when to run."

Mrs. Mills asked, "Is everyone listening?

Run, squirrels, run!"

Kevin said, "Run to a tree, Lucy!"

Lucy ran to a tree.

"Oh, Lucy," said Pam.

"You didn't listen.

We didn't want you to run

to a real tree!"

When the game was over,
everyone went back into school.

Mrs. Mills said, "We are going to see
a play now.

We will go to Room 2."

Lucy was putting her things away.
She was not listening.
When she came back into the room,
no one was there.

"I think everyone went to eat lunch,"
Lucy thought.

Lucy went to get her lunch box.
Then she went to the lunchroom.
But no one was there.
"Where could they be?" she thought.
"I'll have to go back to the room."

Lucy went back to her room.

No one was there.

"What do I do now?" she thought.

Then Mrs. Mills came in.

"Here you are, Lucy!" she said.

"I have looked everywhere for you."

"I went to the lunchroom," said Lucy.

"Where did everyone go?"

"You didn't listen," said Mrs. Mills.

"I said that we were going to see a play.

But now the play may be all over."

Lucy and Mrs. Mills went to Room 2.

"Oh, no!" said Lucy.

"The play *is* over."

"I didn't listen," said Lucy.

"I was too busy putting my things away."

"You are a good worker,
Lucy," said Mrs. Mills.
"But you have to be
a good listener, too."

"From now on, I will not be
too busy to listen!" said Lucy.

What Do You Think?

Can a tree see?

Can a fox box?

Can feet eat?

What Will You Do?

There are many things you could do when you grow up.

Do you like to make things?

Then you may decide to do this.

Do you like to do this?

Then someday
you may do this.

Maybe this is what you like to do.

You may decide to do this.

Maybe this is something
that you like to do.

Someday you could be doing this.

Can a Mouse Really Help?

Rabbit

Lion

Tiger

Mouse

Squirrel

Mouse: Rabbit, look at the game
I found.

It's really fun.

Do you want to play it with me?

Rabbit: No, thank you, Mouse.

I need to do some jumping.

I am going to be in a race.

Mouse: Can I jump with you?

Rabbit: You're too little to jump
with me.

You will get in my way.

Why don't you go and find someone
to play your game with you?

Mouse: Hello there, Squirrel.
Where are you going?

Squirrel: I'm on my way to work.

Mouse: May I go with you?
I could be a big help to you.

Squirrel: You're too little to be a help.

Mouse: I may be little, but I can help.

Squirrel: My work is very important.
I don't want to work with a little mouse.

Tiger: Hello, Mouse.

How good of you to come see me.

Mouse: Oh, no!

I have to get out of here!

I'm getting away from you, Tiger.

You're no fun to be with.

Help! Help!

Someone get me out of here!

Lion: Why are you making
all that noise?

Do you have to shout like that?

Mouse: Oh, good.

It's you, Lion.

I'm shouting for help.

I need to get away from Tiger.

Will you help me?

Lion: What will I get for helping you?

Mouse: If you help me, then someday
I will help you.

Lion: Oh, Mouse, you are really funny.

You're so little!

How could you help me?

Mouse: You will see, Lion.

Lion: OK, Mouse.

I'll see that Tiger

will not get you.

You go now.

Mouse: Thanks for your help, Lion!

Lion: Did you hear what that mouse said to me, Tiger?

She thinks she can help me someday. Isn't that funny?

Tiger: Yes, it is.

She is so little.

There is no way she could help you.

That mouse is really funny!

Tiger: Look out, Lion!

Look out for that net.

Lion: Oh, no, Tiger!

Look at me!

How am I going to get out of here?

Tiger: I'm here, Lion.

I'll get you out.

Tiger: I can't get you out, Lion.
I'll have to get some help.
You wait here for me.

Lion: I *have* to wait here.
I can't get out of this net.

Tiger: I need your help, Squirrel!

Lion is in a net, and I can't get

him out of it.

Squirrel: Can't you see how busy I am?

I'm doing some very important work.

I can't stop now.

Tiger: Come on, Squirrel.

You have to help.

I can't get Lion out myself.

We will get Rabbit to help, too.

Tiger: This isn't working.

We can't get Lion out this way.

Rabbit: What are we going to do?

Squirrel: We have a very big problem.

Mouse: What's going on here?
Why are you making all this noise?

Rabbit: We have a problem, Mouse.
Lion is in that net, and we can't
get him out.

Mouse: Oh, that's no problem.
I'll get him out for you.

Squirrel: Go away, Mouse.
You're too little to help.

Mouse: I can get Lion out of the net.
You wait and see.

Rabbit: Can you really do it, Mouse?

Mouse: Yes, it's no problem for me.

Squirrel: Mouse is really getting Lion out.
Look at her cut that net!

Mouse: All of you help me pull Lion out.

One, two, three, PULL!

Squirrel: We did it!

Lion is out of the net!

Lion: Mouse is the one who really did it.

Thank you, Mouse.

Lion

by MARY ANN HOBERMAN

Look!
A lion!
Mighty beast.
    (Might he
    Bite me
    For a feast?)
Though
I know
He wouldn't dare,
    I'm mighty glad
    He's over there.

Abu Ali and the Coat

by DOROTHY O. VAN WOERKOM

Abu Ali was going to Musa's house
for lunch.

On the way, he stopped to see
his friend Hamid.

"Friend Hamid," he said.

"May I take your coat today?"

"Yes, you may," said Hamid.

"But why do you want it?"

"I need pockets," said Abu Ali.

"And there are many pockets

in your coat."

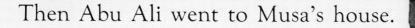

Then Abu Ali went to Musa's house.

"Come in, Ali!" said Musa.
"Lunch is ready!"

"Thank you, Musa," said Abu Ali.
"I'll have some turnip."

Abu Ali took some turnip.
"What good turnip," he said.

"Have some more," said Musa.

Abu Ali took some more turnip.
He put it in his pocket.

"Why did you do that?" Musa asked.

"My coat is hungry," Abu Ali said.

"Have some bread," said Musa.

Abu Ali took some bread.
He put that in a pocket, too.

"Is that for your hungry coat, too?"
asked Musa.

"Oh, yes," said Abu Ali.
"This is a very hungry coat!"

Abu Ali took many more things to eat.

He put one of everything in a pocket
of the coat.

When it was time to go, Abu Ali said,
"Good day, Musa.

Thank you for the good lunch."

"Good day, Ali," said Musa.

"And good day to your coat."

Abu Ali went home.

"I will not have to make dinner today," he said.

"My dinner is in the pockets of this coat."

Abu Ali decided to have

a little sleep.

"I will get into bed now," he said.

Hamid came to Abu Ali's house.

"Friend Ali," said Hamid.

"I need my coat."

But Abu Ali was sleeping.

So Hamid took back his coat.

"Oh, what a good friend Ali is!"
said Hamid.

"He put many good things to eat
in my coat pockets.

Now I will not have to make dinner."

Pockets

by MARY ANN HOBERMAN

Pockets hold things

Pockets hide things

Special private dark inside things.

Pockets save things

Pockets keep things

Secret silent way down deep things.

Books to Enjoy

Am I a Bunny? by Ida DeLage

Mother Bunny and some friends help
Bunny find out that he really is a bunny.

Where Is It? by Tana Hoban

A rabbit looks for a special surprise.

Find the Cat by Elaine Livermore

Help the dog look for the cat.

The cat is hidden in the pictures.

Where Is My Friend?
by Betsy and Guilio Maestro

Many things happen when Harriet looks
for her friend.

Sunshine

MAGAZINE THREE

Contents

Ira Sleeps Over

by BERNARD WABER

I was going to sleep over

at my friend Reggie's house.

It was really going to be fun.

But I had a problem.

It was my sister who thought of it.

She said, "Are you taking

your teddy bear?"

"Taking my teddy bear!" I said.

"To my friend's house?

No, I'm not taking my teddy bear."

And then she said,

"How will it be sleeping

without your teddy bear?

Hmmmmm?"

"It will be OK.

I'll like sleeping

without my teddy bear," I said.

But now, she really had me thinking

about it.

"What if I don't like sleeping
without my teddy bear?" I thought.
"Should I take him?"

"Take him," said my mother.

"Take him," said my father.

"But Reggie will laugh," I said.

"He won't laugh," said my mother.

"He won't laugh," said my father.

"He will laugh," said my sister.

I decided not to take my teddy bear.

After that I went to play with Reggie.

Reggie said, "When you come to my house, we are going to have fun, fun, fun."

"Good," I said, "I can't wait."

"By the way," I asked, "what do you think of teddy bears?"

But Reggie didn't hear me.

"When you sleep over,
we can tell stories," said Reggie.
"We can tell ghost stories."

"Ghost stories?" I asked.

"Yes, ghost stories," said Reggie.

I thought about my teddy bear.
"Will your house be very dark?"
I asked.

"Uh-huh," said Reggie.

"Very, very dark?" I asked.

"Uh-huh," said Reggie.

"By the way," I asked,

"what do you think of teddy bears?"

But then Reggie had to go home.

"See you," said Reggie.

"See you," I said.

I decided to take my teddy bear.

"Good," said my mother.

"Good," said my father.

But my sister said, "Will you tell Reggie your teddy bear's name?
Did you think about how he will laugh at a name like Tah Tah?"

"He won't ask," I said.

"He will ask," she said.

I decided not to take my teddy bear.

It was time to go to Reggie's house.

"Good night," said my mother.

"Good night," said my father.

"Sleep tight," said my sister.

I went over to Reggie's house.

That night we played with everything
in Reggie's room.

Then Reggie's father said,
"Time for bed!"

"Now?" asked Reggie.

"Now," said his father.

We got into bed.

"Now we can tell ghost stories,"
said Reggie.

"Can you tell one?" I asked.

"Uh-huh," said Reggie.

"There was this ghost in a big, dark,
old house.

And every night this ghost made noises.

Ooooh! Ooooooooh! Like that.

And it went looking for someone to scare.

And the ghost was very scary to look at.

Oh, was it scary to look at!"

Reggie stopped.

"Are you scared?" he asked.

"Uh-huh, are you?" I asked.

"What?" asked Reggie.

"Are you scared?" I asked.

"Wait," said Reggie.

"I have to get something."

"What do you have to get?" I asked.

"Oh, something," said Reggie.

Reggie got the something out.
The room was dark, but I could see
what he had.
It looked like a teddy bear.
I looked some more.
It was a teddy bear.

Reggie got back into bed.
"Now, about this ghost . . ." he said.

"Is that your teddy bear?" I asked.

"What, this teddy bear?" asked Reggie.

"Yes, that one," I said.

"Uh-huh," said Reggie.

"Do you sleep with it all of the time?"
I asked.

"Uh-huh," said Reggie.

"What's your teddy bear's name?" I asked.

"You won't laugh?" asked Reggie.

"No, I won't laugh," I said.

"It's Foo Foo," said Reggie.

"Foo Foo?" I asked.

"Uh-huh," said Reggie.

"I have to get something," I said.

"What do you have to get?"
asked Reggie.

"Oh, something,"
I said.

I went back to my house.

"Ira!" everyone said.

"What are you doing here?"

"I decided to take Tah Tah,"
I said.

I went up to my room.

I came back with Tah Tah.

My sister said, "Reggie will laugh.
You'll see how he will laugh."

"He won't laugh," said my mother.

"He won't laugh," said my father.

"He won't laugh," I said.

I came back to Reggie's room.

"I have a teddy bear, too," I said.

"Do you want me to tell you his name?"

I waited, but Reggie said nothing.

I looked at Reggie.

He was sleeping.

"Reggie!" I said.

"You have to tell the end

of the ghost story."

Reggie held his teddy bear tight

and went on sleeping.

And after that —

There was nothing to do after that.

"Good night," I said to Tah Tah.

And I went to sleep, too.

Fuzzy Wuzzy

Fuzzy Wuzzy was a bear,

A bear was Fuzzy Wuzzy.

When Fuzzy Wuzzy lost his hair

He wasn't fuzzy, was he?

The Library

A library is a place
with many, many books.
There are storybooks.
There are books that tell
about real things.
And there are books that tell
how to make things.

Sometimes you can listen to someone
tell a story at the library.
At other times you may see a play.

A library is a fun place to go.

You can take some of the fun home.

You can take home some library books!

Asha's School

by BERYL GRAHAM

Asha lived with her mother, her father, and her sister Layla.

Asha and Layla played school every day.

Layla was the teacher all the time.

Asha liked Layla's school.

Layla helped Asha to make many things
and to play many games.

One day it was time for Layla
to go away to a real school.

Now Asha had no one to play with.

She was very sad.

"Mama, why can't I go to school?"
Asha asked.

"You're too little for school,"
said Mama.

"I want to go to school," thought Asha.
"I don't like being so little."

Mama saw how sad Asha was.

"Asha, do you want to go to the market
with me today?" she asked.

Asha liked the market very much.
There were many things to do there.
So Asha decided to go with Mama.

When Asha and Mama got to the market,
they saw a little girl.

The little girl looked very sad.

Asha went over to her and said,
"Hello, what is your name?"

The little girl said nothing.
She just looked at Asha.

"Maybe I can talk with her," said Mama.

"Jambo," said Mama to the little girl.

"Jambo!" shouted the little girl.
Now she didn't look so sad.

"Is her name Jambo?" asked Asha.

Mama said, "No, Jambo is one way
to say hello."

"Oh, that's why she didn't talk to me,"
said Asha.

"We don't talk the same way."

Mama talked with the little girl.

Then Mama said, "Asha, this is Mosi.

Her mother works in this market.

There is no one for Mosi to play with."

"I will play with you, Mosi,"
said Asha.

Mosi didn't know what Asha had said.

But she could see that Asha wanted

to be her friend.

Asha smiled at Mosi.

"Come on, Mosi," she said.

"We are going to play a game."

Mosi smiled back at Asha.

She didn't know what Asha was saying.

But Mosi could tell that she and Asha

were going to have fun.

Asha and Mosi went over to a man
who had fish for sale.

Asha pointed to a fish and said,
"Fish, Mosi. Say fish."

Mosi looked at the fish.

Then she smiled and said, "Fish."

Then Asha and Mosi ran over to a tree.

Asha pointed to the tree and said,

"Tree, Mosi. Say tree."

"Tree," said Mosi.

Now Mosi could play the game.

Asha pointed to a hen and said,

"Say hen, Mosi."

"Hen!" shouted Mosi.

Just then Mama came back.

"Mama, we are playing school, and I'm the teacher," said Asha.

"I can see that you and Mosi are having fun," said Mama.

"Now every time we come to the market, you and Mosi can play school."

"Good!" said Asha.

"Good!" said Mosi.

168

The Vowels *a, e,* and *i*

Say these words.

Listen for the vowel sound.

hat   am   back

The vowel sound you hear is

the short **a** sound.

Find the words that have

the short **a** sound.

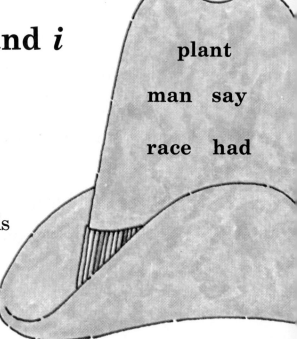

plant

man   say

race   had

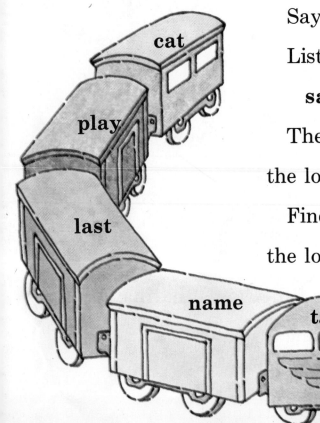

cat

play

last

name

Say these words.

Listen for the vowel sound.

same   way   make

The vowel sound you hear is

the long **a** sound.

Find the words that have

the long **a** sound.

take

169

Say these words.

Listen for the vowel sound.

went   tell   get

The vowel sound you hear is

the short **e** sound.

Find the words that have

the short **e** sound.

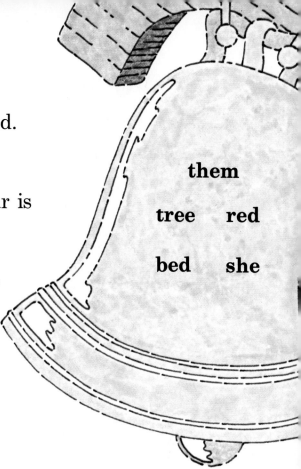

them

tree   red

bed   she

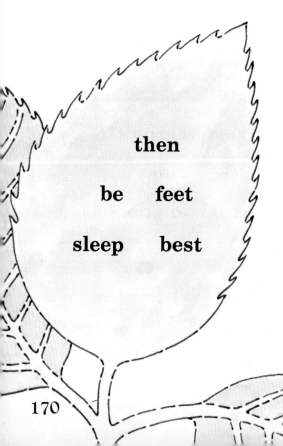

then

be   feet

sleep   best

Say these words.

Listen for the vowel sound.

need   we   see

The vowel sound you hear is

the long **e** sound.

Find the words that have

the long **e** sound.

Say these words.

Listen for the vowel sound.

this   if   swim

The vowel sound you hear is

the short **i** sound.

Find the words that have

the short **i** sound.

smile

win   it

find   big

Say these words.

Listen for the vowel sound.

tight   I   ride

The vowel sound you hear is

the long **i** sound.

Find the words that have

the long **i** sound.

night

time

did

pig

like

Help Tina

Can you help Tina find her dog?

1. It is a big dog.

2. It is a red dog.

3. It is a dog that is eating.

Buzzy Bear and the Rainbow

by DOROTHY MARINO

One day Buzzy Bear ran out to play.
It had just stopped raining.

Buzzy stopped by a tree.
"Oh, look!" he said to a bird
in the tree.
"There is a rainbow."

"Yes," said the bird.

"I hear there is gold at the end
of a rainbow."

Buzzy didn't wait to hear more.
He ran home.
Mother and Father Bear were looking
at the rainbow, too.

Buzzy ran into the house
to get a big pot.

When he came back out, he said,
"I'm going to get the gold."
Then he ran on.

"That's just a story,"
called Mother Bear.

"We don't need gold,"
called Father Bear.

175

Buzzy just ran on.

He could see the end of the rainbow
by a big rock.

When Buzzy got to the big rock,
he could not see the rainbow.

A squirrel was there.

"I'm looking for the end of the rainbow,"
said Buzzy to the squirrel.

"Look at the little trees over there,"
said the squirrel.

"There's the end of the rainbow."

Buzzy ran to find it.

The squirrel called to him,
"If you're looking for the gold,
that's just a story."

Buzzy just ran on.
When he got to the little trees,
he could not see the rainbow.
A rabbit was there.

"I'm looking for the end
of the rainbow," said Buzzy
to the rabbit.

"See that grass over there?"
the rabbit asked.
"There's the end of the rainbow."

Buzzy ran to find it.

The rabbit called to him,
"If you're looking for the gold,
that's just a story."

178

Buzzy just ran on.

When he got to the grass,

he could not see the rainbow.

A chipmunk was there.

"I'm looking for the end

of the rainbow," said Buzzy

to the chipmunk.

"Look at that big tree over there,"

said the chipmunk.

"There's the end of the rainbow."

Buzzy ran to find it.

The chipmunk called to him,
"If you're looking for the gold,
that's just a story."

Buzzy just ran on.
When he got to the tree,
Buzzy looked all over.
There was no rainbow.

"This really must be the end
of the rainbow!" he said.

Buzzy went up the tree.

Then he stopped.

There was a big hole in the tree.

Buzzy looked in.

"I found it!" he shouted.

"I found the gold . . . and I like it."

Buzzy put the gold into the big pot.

Then he came down the tree.

"I'll run home now," thought Buzzy.

"I found the gold," Buzzy called
to the chipmunk.

"Wait, let me see," called the chipmunk.

Buzzy just ran on.
The chipmunk ran after Buzzy.

"I found the gold," Buzzy called
to the rabbit.

"Wait, let me see," called the rabbit.

Buzzy just ran on.
The rabbit ran after Buzzy
and the chipmunk.

"I found the gold," Buzzy called
to the squirrel.

"Wait, let me see," called the squirrel.

Buzzy just ran on.
The squirrel ran after Buzzy
and the chipmunk and the rabbit.

They all ran to Buzzy's house.

Buzzy Bear held up the pot
for Mother Bear to see.

"Look, Mother," he said.

"There really was gold at the end
of the rainbow."

They all looked into the pot.

"It's honey!" shouted Father Bear.
"Buzzy found honey at the end
of the rainbow!"

Buzzy Bear called the little bird
from the tree.
Then Mother Bear asked
all of Buzzy's friends to eat dinner
with them.

"I'll make pancakes for dinner,"
Mother Bear said.

· They put honey on the pancakes.
"My, they are good," they all said.

Father Bear said, "We don't need
real gold.
The gold Buzzy found is much better."

Bears

by ELIZABETH COATSWORTH

Bears have few cares.

When the wind blows cold

and the snow drifts deep,

they sleep

and sleep

and sleep

and sleep.

Books to Enjoy

And I Mean It, Stanley

by Crosby Bonsall

Read this book and find out who
Stanley is.

Bedtime for Bears by Adelaide Holl

The little bear isn't ready for bed.

He wants to wait and see the moon.

Harriet Goes to the Circus

by Betsy and Guilio Maestro

Harriet is the first to get in line.

She ends up being last, but finds

that being last isn't bad after all.

Odd One Out by Rodney Peppe

Find the funny thing in each picture.

Bernard Waber; p. 154, Marc Brown; pp. 155-157, Tomie de Paola; pp. 158-168, Freya Tanz; pp. 169-171, Dorothea Sierra; p. 172, Ann Iosa; pp. 173-187, Maggie Swanson; p. 188, Jerry Pinkney.

Photographers: p. 44(top), Calvin Larsen/Photo Researchers, Inc.; p. 44(bottom), S. Rannels/Grant Heilman; p. 45(top), Laura Riley/ Bruce Coleman, Inc.; p. 45(bottom), Hans Reinhard/Bruce Coleman, Inc.; p. 46, Deidra Stead; pp. 97-100, Deidra Stead; p. 117, Tom McHugh/Photo Researchers, Inc.

Book cover, title page, and magazine covers by Tomie de Paola. *Fabric design:* Copyright 1975 V.I.P., a Division of Cranston Print Works Company.

Sounds You Know

b c d f g h j k l m n p r s t w v x y

ch   sh   th   c pencil

fl   fr   pl   st   sw

___ ch   ___ sh   ___ th   ___ st

New Sounds

kn   br   gr   sc   sl

ai

ay

oo

___ y

Turn the page.

More New Sounds

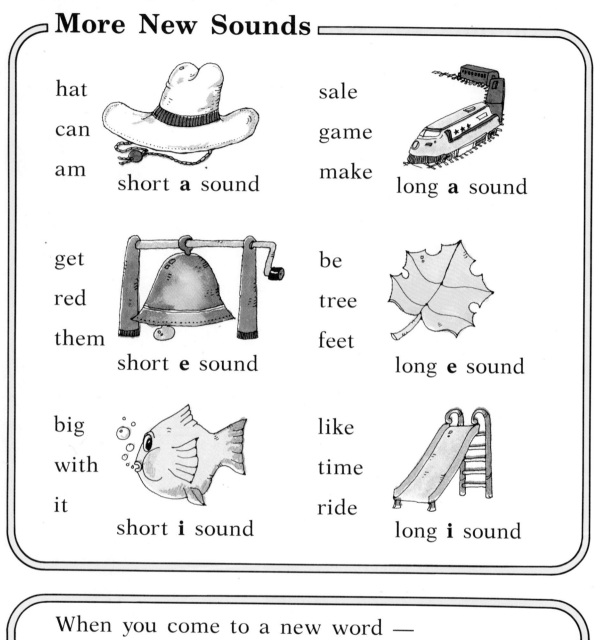

hat
can
am

short **a** sound

sale
game
make

long **a** sound

get
red
them

short **e** sound

be
tree
feet

long **e** sound

big
with
it

short **i** sound

like
time
ride

long **i** sound

When you come to a new word —

Read to the end of the sentence.

Think about what the words are saying.

Think about the sounds for letters.